SO-ABC-273

a collection of traditional lullabies
each sung in its original language and in English
(Multicultural activities included)

Music arranged by Sara Jordan

Produced and Published by
Sara Jordan Publishing
a division of
℗© MCMXCVI Jordan Music Productions Inc.
(SOCAN)

ISBN: 978-1-895523-78-2

Acknowledgments

Producer, arranger - Sara Jordan

Many thanks to the following singers: Fern Dworkin (Yiddish), Peter Lovrick (Mandarin), Dominique Show (Lingala), Takako Lordly (Japanese), André Busigin (Russian), Peter LeBuis (French), Mary Lou Sicoly (Italian), Bergi Weinberger (German), Margaret Chlebowski (Polish), Mary Paz Young (Spanish). Singing in English: Peter LeBuis and Jennifer Moore.

Recording Engineer - Mark Shannon, Sound Image Productions

Copy editing - Kay Oxford

Layout - Ruxandra Kovacs, Darryl Taylor, Mike Hearn

Cover Design - Campbell Creative Services

Illustrations - Glen Wyand and Tanya Grimaldi (Origami)

Special thanks to Mark Shannon for his incredible programming of arrangements.

Recorded and mixed - Sound Image Productions
Toronto, Ontario

For further information contact:

Jordan Music Productions Inc.
M.P.O. Box 490
Niagara Falls, NY
U.S.A. 14302-0490

Jordan Music Productions Inc.
Station M, Box 160
Toronto, Ontario
Canada M6S 4T3

Internet: www.SongsThatTeach.com
e-mail: sjordan@sara-jordan.com
Telephone: (800) 567-7733

For kids around the world

who are all very special.

Table of Contents

Hints for Teachers and Parents

Mother love is universal and it survives in folk lullabies the world over. Lullabies are most often passed down from generation to generation and from one country to another. The words may change a little and the melody vary slightly, but the meaning and essence of each lullaby remain intact.

Parents the world over have sung lullabies to their young. They sing songs of peace and tranquillity and of great hope for the child's future.

These songs have been compiled with great hope too; a hope for a growing sense of peace, acceptance, tolerance and compassion within our schools and communities.

Music, the universal language, is now noted to be one of the Seven Multiple Intelligences thanks to research by Harvard professor and author, Howard Gardner. Daniel Goleman, in his book *Emotional Intelligence*, also sees music as an important vehicle in developing our expression of intelligence.

It is our hope that you use the collection of lullabies here, to boost knowledge, interest in learning, linguistics and fun across the curriculum.

A few ways to use *Lullabies Around the World:*

The lullabies and activities in this kit can be used to enrich learning in many ways.

Phonetic pronunciation of each lullaby in a foreign language is included, so that students can sing along with the lullabies.

The complement of instrumental tracks can be used as a type of "test" when students feel that they can perform one or more of the lullabies by heart. It also comes in very handy for parent night/school performances.

Varied cultural activities accompanying each lullaby can be found in this lyrics book. Some of the activities take a little more time than others. For example, Kasperle, the German puppet, made out of paper mâché, may take as long as a week to make. The activities here, along with the lullabies, could be used as the format for a very entertaining multicultural evening.

A recipe is included, here, for Tiramisu, an Italian cake. What recipes can students contribute of favorite foods from their own homeland?

To further enhance the activities included, have students plot out the various countries on a large map on your classroom wall. Have them create a scrapbook collection of articles and pictures of the various cultures and countries included here.

Bai, Bai, Bai, Bai

Bai, bai, bai, bai,
Báyu, Detusku mayú!
Bai, bai, bai, bai,
Báyu, Detusku mayú!
Shta na górki, na goryé,
O visyénnei, o poryé,
Ptíchki Bozhiye payút,
F tyómnam lyési gnyózda vyut.

Bai, bai, bai, bai,
Bayu, Orchid, little dear.
Bai, bai, bai, bai,
Bayu, Orchid, little dear.
On the hillside in the spring,
Birds of heaven sweetly sing,
Seeking for their young what's best
In the forest dark they nest.

Russian Activity
- Coloring Easter Eggs -

In Russia, eggs are colored for the Easter Holiday to celebrate this special time.

All you need to start off are hard boiled eggs, non-toxic egg dye, and crayons.

Take a hard boiled egg, and dip it, using a large spoon or ladel, into a container with one color of dye dissolved in the water.

Hint: Start with lighter colors, like yellow, and work your way to darker colors.

After leaving the egg in the dye for approximately 5 minutes, take it out using your spoon and let it dry.

Using a crayon (same color as the dye), draw a design on the egg.

Flowers are often drawn on Russian eggs! Repeat the procedure, each time using a slightly darker color of dye (and crayon). When you are finished, an adult should place the eggs in a warm oven on a tray, so that the wax can melt off.

Duérmete Mi Niño

Duérmete mi niño.
Duérmete solito.
Qué cuando te despiertes,
Te daré atolito.

Duérmete mi niño.
Duérmete mi sol.
Duérmete pedazo,
De mi corazón.

Go to sleep my baby.
Go to sleep and dream,
for when you awaken
you shall have some cream.

Go to sleep my baby.
Go to sleep my sunshine.
You will always be
in this heart of mine.

Mexican Activity
- Ojo de Dios -

The Ojo de Dios comes originally from the Huichol Indians of Mexico. Its red, yellow and blue colors are said to protect children and make them as strong as Aztecs and to help the crops.

You will need (per child):
- Pieces of red, yellow and blue 3 ply yarn
  (It's best for young children if these are
  tied together at the onset.)
- 2 popsicle sticks tied into a cross
- A pair of small scissors

 Tie a knot around the two sticks, close to the center.

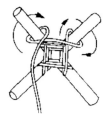 Move in a circle, wrapping the yarn over each stick in succession.

 Finish off by tying a knot.

Rozinkes mit Mandlen

In dem bays hamikdosh,

In a vinkl chayder

Zitzt di almone bas Tziyon aley.

Ir ben yochidl Yidele vigt si k'seyder.

Un zingt im tzum shlofen a lidele sheyn.

Unter Yidele's vigele

Shteyt a klor veis tzigele.

Dos tzigele is geforen handlen;

Dos vet zein dein beruf.

Rozinkes mit mandlen.

Shlof-zhe Yidele, shlof.

In the room of the temple,

In a cosy corner

There sits a widow all alone.

With her only little child she rocks gently

While singing a lovely lullaby.

"And beneath the cradle

There's a little pure white goat,

The little goat went out looking

Just as you'll do some day,

Bringing raisins and almonds.

Sleep, sweet baby, sleep."

The Yiddish language was developed by Jews in Germany perhaps as early as the 9th century. Yiddish is written using the Hebrew alphabet. As Jews migrated from Germany, it became the normal Jewish vernacular in Europe and America.

Rozinkes mit Mandlen is one of the most famous Yiddish lullabies. It was written by the founder of modern Yiddish theatre, Abraham Goldfaden, in 1880 and is part of a song from the operetta 'Shulamis'.

Jewish Activity
- Dreidel Pattern -

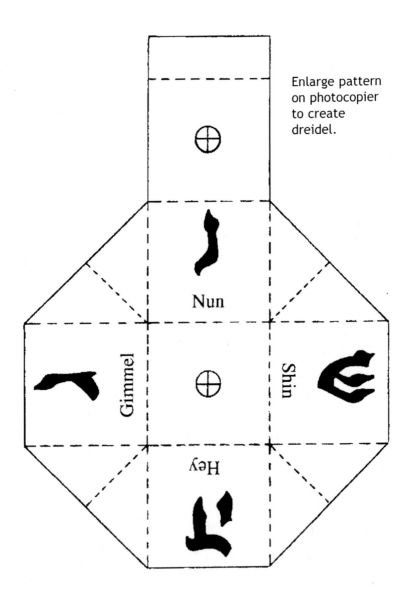

Enlarge pattern on photocopier to create dreidel.

Lullabies Around the World © MCMXCVI Sara Jordan Publishing

Jewish Activity
- Making a Dreidel -

A dreidel is a toy that Jewish children play with during the eight day festival of Chanukkah.

Materials needed:
- unsharpened pencil• scissors• glue, markers
- a piece of heavy paper or cardboard

Making the dreidel:

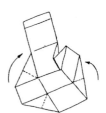

- Photocopy the dreidel pattern onto heavy paper.
- Fold the pattern on all dotted lines to form a dreidel.
- Put glue on the tabs or tape them.

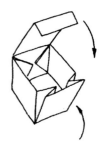

- Cut out four cardboard circles of about 2 inches (5 cm) in diameter for each player.
- Each player should draw the four letters, one on each circle.
- Insert the pencil in the marked hole.

Playing the game:
- Each player should take turns spinning the dreidel.
- See what side it lands on, and take the corresponding circle and place it in the middle.
- The game is won by the first person to place all their circles in the middle.

Fi la nana, e mi bel fiol

Fi la nana, e mi bel fiol,
Fi la nana, e mi bel fiol,
Fa si la nana.
Fa si la nana.

Dormi ben, e mi bel fiol,
Dormi ben, e mi bel fiol,
Fa si la nana.
Fa si la nana.

Hush-a-bye, my lovely child,
Hush-a-bye, my lovely child,
Hush, hush and go to sleep.
Hush, hush and go to sleep.

Sleep well, my lovely child,
Sleep well, my lovely child,
Hush, hush and go to sleep.
Hush, hush and go to sleep.

Italian Activity
- Tiramisu Cake -

Tiramisu cake is an Italian cake which originated in Puglia - a region in the south part of Italy.

Ingredients:

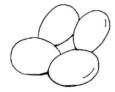

4 eggs yolks

1 cup sugar

9 ounces (250g) cream

20 ounces (475g) Mascarpone cheese
(Philadelphia cream cheese can be substituted)

2 packages of lady finger cookies

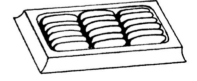

Mix the egg yolks and sugar. Add the Mascarpone cheese to the batter. Whip the whipping cream. Fold into batter.

Italian Activity
- Making the Cake -

Dip the cookies into a cup of
coffee briefly until they are
wet.

Form a layer of them in
bottom of disposible cake tin.
Add layer of mixture. Repeat
layer of cookies. Top off with
layer of mixture. Refrigerate.

To serve:
Cut open the disposable pan
and slice when cold.

*Thanks to Caterina Pepe of the Progress Bakery (an
Italian bakery in Toronto) for this wonderful recipe.*

Yao Yah Yao

sing twice:
> Yao yah yao
> Yao yah yao
> Bao bao huai jung shuay
> Yao ni jang da
> Yo liao sheewang
> Bao bao kuai jang da
> Bao bao kuai jang da

sing twice:
> *Rock-a-bye.*
> *Rock-a-bye.*
> *Sleep, you're safe with me.*
> *Rock you*
> *'til you're big,*
> *Rock you*
> *'til you're strong,*
> *Baby grow up soon.*
> *Baby grow up soon.*

Yao Yah Yao in Mandarin

搖 籃 曲

搖　呀　搖　　　　　搖　呀　搖

寶 寶 懷 中 睡　　　搖　你　長　大

有　　　希 望　寶 寶 快 長 大

寶 寶 快 長 大

Lullabies Around the World　© MCMXCVI　Sara Jordan Publishing

Chinese Activity
- Chinese Jump Rope -

Rules for playing

Chinese children first played Jump Rope in the 7th century.

The "jump rope" is a piece of elastic about 72 inches (1.8 meters) long, with the ends tied together.

The game is played by having two people face each other standing inside the rope. The rope is around their ankles. It is stretched tightly, forming two parallel jumping lines. A third person stands outside the rope, ready to jump in. It is decided how the person must jump by all three players.

A mistake is made when the jumper trips over the rope while jumping, or when they do not jump in the correct position. When a mistake is made, the next person does the jumping, and the previous jumper takes that person's position.

Chinese Jump Rope is a game played for fun, though you can make it competitive if you choose to. Enjoy!

Oj, Lu Lu

Phonetic pronunciation of the Polish is given here.

Oi lu lu lu lu lu, Kolibka z marmooroo,
Pielushki zrabechku, lulie aniowedgku.

chorus:
Lu-lu, lu-lu-lu, lu-lu, lu-lu-lu,
Lu-lu, lu-lu-lu, lu-lu, lu-lu-lu.

Chervone yagody spadayo dow vody,
Yuzem pshekonany, Ze nie mam urody

chorus:

Hotch urody nie mam,
Myuntku nieviele,
E tak vas nie prosche,
O neets pshayiachele.

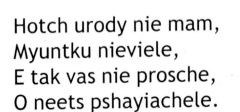

OJ, LU LU

Oj lu lu lu lu lu, Kolibka z marmuru,
Pieluszki zrąbeczku, lulaj anioleczku.
Lu-lu, lu-lu-lu, lu-lu, lu-lu-lu,
Lu-lu, lu-lu-lu, lu-lu, lu-lu.

Czerwone jagody spadają do wody,
Ja żem przekonany, Ze nie mam urody
Lu-lu, lu-lu-lu, lu-lu, lu-lu,
Lu-lu, lu-lu-lu, lu-lu, lu-lu.

Choć urody nie mam, Majątku nie wiele,
I tak was nie proszę, O nic przyjaciele.
Lu-lu, lu-lu-lu, lu-lu, lu-lu-lu,
Lu-lu, lu-lu-lu, lu-lu, lu-lu.

Polish spelling

chorus:

Oi lu lu lu lu lu. No cradle of marble,
No pillows of lace for you, my darling.

chorus:

Splashing in the water, fall the red berries.
You my little baby, you make me so merry.

chorus:

Though I own few things,
I'll not ever need more,
I have you my darling
You are what I've prayed for.

chorus:

Polish Activity
- Decorative Paper Chains -

The Christmas tree is very important to Polish people and almost all of their decorations are handmade. Try your hand at these simple chains to decorate your festive season.

Steps:

Cut identical strips of paper of various colors. Glue the ends together.

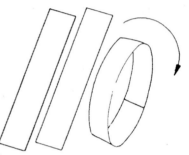

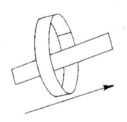 

Link the chains together as shown.

Enjoy your chain!

 Lullabies Around the World © MCMXCVI Sara Jordan Publishing

Schlaf, Kindlein, Schlaf

Schlaf, Kindlein, schlaf.
Der Vater hüt't die Schaf.
Die Mutter schüttelt's Bäumelein,
Da fällt herab ein Träumelein.
Schlaf, Kindlein, schlaf!

Schlaf, Kindlein, schlaf.
Am Himmel ziehn die Schaf.
Die Sternlein sind die Lämmerlein,
Der Mond, der ist das Schäferlein.
Schlaf, Kindlein, schlaf!

Schlaf, Kindlein, schlaf.
So schenk' ich dir ein Schaf.
Mit einer goldnen Schelle fein,
Das soll dein Spielgeselle sein.
Schlaf, Kindlein, schlaf.

Sleep, Baby, sleep.
Your father tends the sheep.
Your mother shakes the branches small,
Lovely dreams in showers fall.
Sleep, Baby, sleep.

Sleep, Baby, sleep.
Across the heavens move the sheep.
The little stars are lambs, I guess,
And the moon is the shepherdess.
Sleep, Baby, sleep.

Sleep, Baby, sleep.
I'll give to you a sheep.
And it shall have a bell of gold
For you to play with and to hold.
Sleep, Baby, sleep.

This is one of the most famous lullabies in the world. Johannes Brahms once did an arrangement of it for Schumann's children and Wagner incorporated it into his opera Siegfried-Idyl (written as a birthday gift for his wife and first performed in 1870).

German Activity
- Paper Mâché -
Kasperle, Germany's Favorite Puppet

You will need:

Newspaper, masking tape, white glue, white and colored paints, 3 popsicle sticks, scraps of fabric cut into strips, construction paper.

Easy Steps:

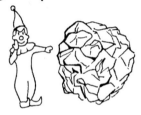

• Crumple a double newspaper page into a ball

• Sculpt the head with masking tape

• Leave a hole at the bottom for the neck

• Push the newspaper into the head

• Leave room for the popsicle stick that will be glued inside later.

Hole

- Soak newspaper strips in the paper mâché solution

- Cover head with 4 layers of strips

- Make eyes, nose and ears by crumpling up small balls of paper mâché

- Cover these with two layers of small strips

- Allow head to dry overnight

- Start by painting entire head with 2 coats of white paint

- Now paint over features with colored paint

- Roll a sheet of construction paper into a cone and fasten it with scotch tape for his hat

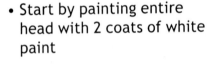

- Tape two popsicle sticks lengthwise to make his body

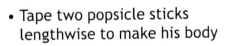

- Tape another stick across the top stick into a cross shape for the "arms"

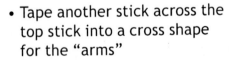

- Glue the cone hat to Kasperle's head

- Glue the popsicle sticks, the "body," onto Kasperle's neck

- Let dry overnight

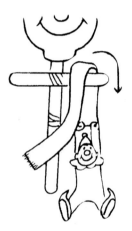

- Cover the popsicle sticks by tying the fabric strips along the length of the "arms"

- Tie a bow around his neck to hide the joint between his head and body

- Enjoy your Kasperle!

Bébé kolela te

This lullaby is in Lingala, one of the native languages of the Democratic Republic of Congo. Lingala is spoken in Congo's capital, Kinshasa. It is a derivative of the French language.

Ye ye
Ye ye
Ye eh eh eh ye ye

Bébé moke
Alelaka te
Soki aleli
Pesa biberon

chorus:

Ye eh eh eh ye ye
Ye ye
Ye ye
Ye eh eh eh ye ye

Muana moke
Alelaka te
Soki aleli
Okende zandote

chorus:

Bébé moke
Alelaka te
Soki aleli
Ayoki pongi

chorus:

Little babies
never cry.
If they cry
give them their bottles.

chorus:

Little babies
never cry.
If they cry
you will not go shopping.

chorus:

Little babies
never cry.
If they cry
they are sleepy.

chorus:

Activity from Congo
- Weaving a Basket -

This activity is very popular in Africa. It is passed down from generation to generation.

Materials that you need:

Variously colored raffia (long strips of colored paper may also be used), glue, round cartons of any size and a pair of scissors

- First you start by cutting the round carton into strips that are approximately 3/4 inches wide.

- Make sure that you start cutting from about 2 inches from the bottom of the carton.
- As well, to be able to weave, the carton must be cut into an uneven number of strips.

- Use the illustration at the side to help you with the weaving pattern.

- Enjoy making the basket, and don't forget that it is also useful. You can always use it to store stuff!

Edo Komoriuta
(Edo Lullaby)

Nen nen kororiyo okororiyo
Boyawa yoikoda nenneshina

Boyano komoriwa dokoe it ta
Anoyama koete satoe it ta

Sato no miyage ni nani morata
Denden taikoni sho no fue
Sho no fue

日本古謡／ハハ澤第孝羅曲

江戸子守唄

ねんねんころりよ　おころりよ
ぼうやは良い子だ　ねんねしな

ぼうやのおもりは　どこへいった
あの山越えて　里へいった

里のみやげに　なにもろた
でんでんだいこに　しょうの笛

Sleep, sleep,
little one, sleep.
You're a good baby,
now go to sleep.

Do you know
where your nurse has gone?
Gone to her village
she won't be long.

What will she bring baby
when she does come?
A flute so lovely
and a thunderous drum.
And a thunderous drum.

Japanese Activity
- Origami -

Folding squares of colored paper into different shapes is a very popular activity for kids in Japan. This is called origami. Here are some instructions to make a paper crane. Any piece of bright paper can be used, and we recommend wrapping paper. Your piece of paper should be approximately 5.5 inches by 5.5 inches.

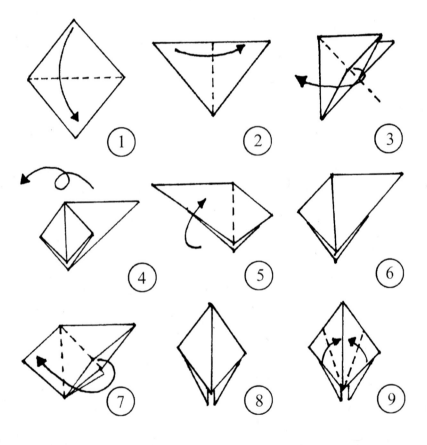

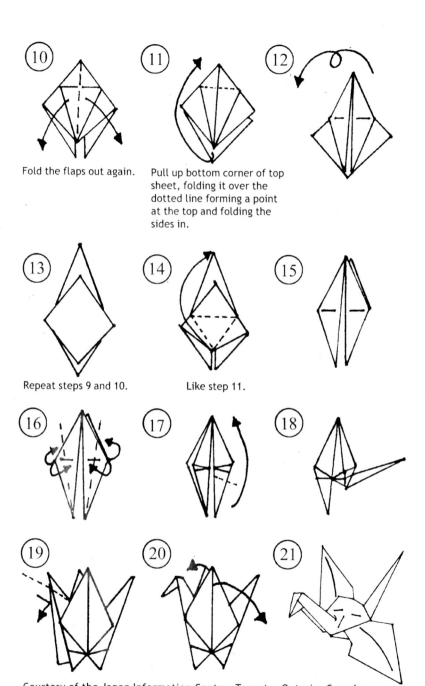

10 Fold the flaps out again.

11 Pull up bottom corner of top sheet, folding it over the dotted line forming a point at the top and folding the sides in.

12

13 Repeat steps 9 and 10.

14 Like step 11.

15

16

17

18

19

20

21

Courtesy of the Japan Information Center, Toronto, Ontario, Canada

C'est la poulette grise

C'est la poulette grise
Qui pond dans l'église,

refrain:

Elle va pondre un petit coco
Pour son petit qui va fair dodiche.
Elle va pondre un petit coco
Pour son petit qui va fair dodo.
Dodiche, dodo.

C'est la poulette brune
Qui pond dans la lune.

refrain:

C'est la poulette blanche
Qui pond dans les branches.

refrain:

There is a gray hen
Who lays in the church.

chorus:

She will lay a pretty little egg
For her little one who is going to sleep.
She will lay a pretty little egg
For her little one who is going to sleep.
Sleep, baby sleep.

There is a little brown hen
Who lays in the moon.

chorus:

There is a little white hen
Who lays in the branches.

chorus:

French-Canadian Activity
- Educational Hopscotch -

- To play the game you must start by drawing the hopscotch on the ground with chalk. Use the illustration here as a guide.

- You begin to play by stepping with 2 feet in the squares marked with numbers 1 and 2.

- You do the same for numbers 3 and 4.

- You then step with only one foot on number 5.

- Then you use two feet for numbers 6 and 7, stepping on both of them at the same time.

- Then you use one foot again for number 8 and two feet for numbers 9 and 10, as you did for 1 and 2.

- You then do the same, but go backwards.

- For your second turn you must do the same, but this time you must call out what number you are stepping on. If you make a mistake you must start over.

- The first to finish is the winner!

French-Canadian Activity
- Educational Hopscotch -

- This time you jump the same way you did the first time.

- The difference this time is that you must say the letters instead of the numbers.

- Another way of playing is that when you call out the letters you must also make up words that start with the letter.

(Sometimes it may be difficult to think of a word with a specific letter, so when you have a choice of a couple of letters pick only one with which to make up a word.)

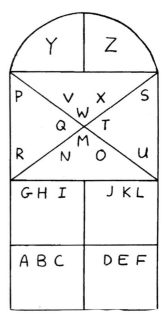

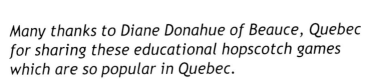

Many thanks to Diane Donahue of Beauce, Quebec for sharing these educational hopscotch games which are so popular in Quebec.

Mocking Bird

Hush, little baby.
Don't say a word.
Mama's going to buy you
   a mocking bird.

And if that mocking bird won't sing,
Mama's going to buy you
   a diamond ring.

If that diamond ring turns brass,
Mama's going to buy you
   a looking glass.

If that looking glass gets broke,
Mama's going to buy you
   a billy goat.

If that billy goat won't pull,
Mama's going to you
    a cart and bull.

If that cart and bull turns over,
Mama's going to buy
    a dog named Rover.

If that dog named Rover won't bark,
Mama's going to buy you
    a horse and cart

If that horse and cart falls down,
You'll still be the sweetest one in town.

Traditional American Activity
- Making a Quilt -

Quilting has been a popular and useful pastime in America for hundreds of years. In the colonial times, neighbors used to gather and work together on one quilt. A quilt may be used for decoration, or as a useful covering to have around the house.

To emulate a quilt using paper, have the children start by giving them each a piece of paper of about 8 inches (20 cm) by 8 inches (20 cm).

The children should then use paint, markers, paper scraps or crayons to color in the piece of paper any way they want. (You may want to use a specific theme throughout the quilt.)

All the squares should then be assembled either on the wall or on a much larger piece of paper.

Special Sources and Resources

Toronto, Canada, one of the most culturally diverse cities in the world, has always been a wonderful place to live. This project could never have been possible without the generosity of so many individuals and associations.

Many thanks to these fine people and resources.

Trudy Booth, Enya and André Busigan, Diane Donahue, Willy Hajek, Waltraud Huettenschmidt, Yurike Kashibe, Peter Lovrick, Kay Oxford, Caterina Pepe, Paula de Ronde, Dominque Show, Pina, Robert Wagner, Kim Yamamoto, The Friedrich Schiller Deutsche Schule and Steve Kennedy of the Japanese Information Centre in Toronto, Canada.

Ask your retailer about other excellent audio programs by teacher, Sara Jordan

Bilingual Preschool™

Jump-start learning for preschoolers as they sing and participate in these bilingual songs and games including I Spy, Follow the Leader and Mind Your Manners. This kit teaches: names of animals, counting, directions, polite expressions, places in the community, and counting (cardinal and ordinal numbers). Sung by native speakers, these bilingual songs are a perfect introduction to the new language.
ENGLISH-FRENCH and ENGLISH-SPANISH

Bilingual Songs™ Volumes 1-4

*** Parents' Choice Award Winner! ***

The perfect way to have fun while acquiring a second language. This series teaches the basic alphabet, counting to 100, days of the week, months of the year, colors, food, animals, parts of the body, clothing, family members, emotions, places in the community and the countryside, measurement, opposites, greetings, gender, articles, plural forms of nouns, adjectives, pronouns, adverbs of frequency, question words and much more!
ENGLISH-FRENCH and ENGLISH-SPANISH

Songs and Activities for Early Learners™

Dynamic songs teach the alphabet, counting, parts of the body, members of the family, colors, shapes, fruit and more. Helps students of all ages to learn basic vocabulary easily. The kit includes a lyrics book with activities which teachers may reproduce for their classes.
IN ENGLISH, FRENCH OR SPANISH

Thematic Songs for Learning Language™

Delightful collection of songs and activities teaching salutations, rooms of the house, pets, meals, food and silverware, transportation, communication, parts of the body, clothing, weather and prepositions. Great for ESL classes. The kit includes a lyrics book with activities which teachers may reproduce for their classes.
IN ENGLISH, FRENCH OR SPANISH

Reading Readiness™ Songs

Packaged with a lyrics book which includes helpful hints for parents and teachers. This great introduction to reading uses both phonetic and whole language approaches. Topics covered include the alphabet, vowels, consonants, telling time, days of the week, seasons, the environment and more!
VERSIONS IN ENGLISH, FRENCH OR SPANISH

Grammar Grooves vol.1™

Ten songs that teach about nouns, pronouns, adjectives, verbs, tenses, adverbs and punctuation. Activities and puzzles, which may be reproduced, are included in the lyrics book to help reinforce learning even further. A complement of music tracks to the 10 songs is included for karaoke performances. Also great for music night productions.
IN ENGLISH, FRENCH OR SPANISH

Funky Phonics®: Learn to Read Volumes 1-4

Blending the best in educational research and practice, Sara Jordan's four part series provides students with the strategies needed to decode words through rhyming, blending and segmenting. Teachers and parents love the lessons while children will find the catchy, toe-tapping tunes fun.
IN ENGLISH

Singing Sight Words Volumes 1-4

This collection of fun songs builds a solid foundation for all beginning readers. By incorporating Dolch sight words into memorable and catchy melodies, early readers are quickly able to recognize the more common and basic words found in age-appropriate literature. IN ENGLISH

Lullabies Around the World

*** Parents'   Choice Award Winner! ***

Traditional lullabies sung by native singers with translated verses in English. Multicultural activities are included in the lyrics book. Includes a complement of music tracks for class performances.
Pre-K - Grade 3 11 DIFFERENT LANGUAGES

The Math Unplugged™ Series

Available for Addition, Subtraction, Division and Multiplication. Tuneful songs teach kids the basic math facts. Repetitive, musical and fun. A great resource. Each audio kit includes a lyrics book with worksheet pages which may be reproduced.
IN ENGLISH

Check out these great Resource Books full of reproducible activities and exercises for the classroom.

Bilingual Kids™ Volumes 1-4

Reproducible, black-line, thematic lessons and exercises, based on *Bilingual Songs*, teach the basic alphabet, counting to 100, days of the week, months of the year, colors, food, animals, parts of the body, clothing, family members, emotions, places in the community and the countryside, measurement, opposites, greetings, gender, articles, plural forms of nouns, adjectives, pronouns, adverbs of frequency, question words and much more! ENGLISH-FRENCH and ENGLISH-SPANISH

Funky Phonics®: Learn to Read Volumes 1-4

Reproducible, black-line, thematic lessons and exercises, based on the *Funky Phonics®: Learn to Read* audio series, is a structured program providing students with the strategies needed to decode words. Teachers, parents and beginning readers love the lessons, hands on activities and reproducible worksheets.
IN ENGLISH

Learning Sight Words Volumes 1-4

This four-part series of 64 page, reproducible, resource/ activity books teaches students 300 of the most commonly used sight words. The words are presented in order of frequency and are based on the 200 most frequently used service words compiled by Edward William Dolch, Ph.D., and the related list of 95 high-frequency nouns. It is estimated that 50-75% of all words used in school books, library books, newspapers and magazines are included in the Dolch Basic Sight Vocabulary. This series can be used independently or in tandem with the audio/book series Singing Sight Words. IN ENGLISH

Please visit our English and Spanish websites, great meeting places for kids, teachers and parents on the Internet.
www.SongsThatTeach.com
www.AprendeCantando.com
For help finding a retailer near you contact
Sara Jordan Publishing 1-800-567-7733